This book is an instant waypoint on my return to the revelation: if nothing else, my tears have a place where they belong—mixed into the dust of others.

- Wilmer Wilson IV

Dust has an elemental fetish and I am here for it. Part post-apocalyptic kink manual, part poetic sexual reckoning at the end of the world when humanity has been wiped off the face of the planet, LA writes for the future that is already here. It terrifies me and helps me understand myself better.

- Callum Angus

Dust is a thrilling provocation. It starts in a cave and weaves through treacherous subterranean passages before bursting through the floor made by our intrinsic urges of erotic and death. In focusing on time yet halting its expansion, LA Warman lights the way into the very ground through her hypnotic voice, equal parts soothing and heartache.

- Cole Lu

If the only language is the tangle-suck of gnarled clit-slash-screech-and-careening, with Warman, we are walking wretchedly together towards what-is-next vs. what-it-was-slash-what-it-is. Built from the survival of a split with knowing, Warman rubs, swallows, and takes us to a salty shape-shifting precipice: What is it to be extinct, desired, inhabited, evacuated, and exhumed by another?

Read this timeless hot, spatial, bodily, and pain-soaked durational performance that takes its form as a solo, duet and a collective concert disguised as their second book. Warman's sex unfurls militant mourning and survival as an echo into the end of time.

- Julie Tolentino

DUST by L.A. Warman © 2022

Copy edited by Emma Burgess-Olson & Fani Avramopoulou

Edited by Tamara Faith Berger & Mitch Anzuoni

Author photo by Tyler Jones

Published by Inpatient Press, NYC 2022

DUST

L.A. Warman

For Yulan who taught me eternal love.

For Chelsea, Natalia, Wilmer, and Husna.

The hole in the wall.

I mean rock. A hole in the rock.

Pumice, ash, tuff.
The color of
The color of
The color of sand.
And the color of my body and the color of her body and the
color of dust.
The color of orange.
The color of red.

The stratification.

The path.
The path led us to the cave.
The cave with black on the ceiling.
The cave occupied for thousands of years.
This black is the black of fire.
Of after fire.
Of people.
In the cave.
Lighting a fire and looking out.
The most beautiful view.

The feeling of being alone.
Of being with her and the fire and the cave.

The cave is room enough for both of us but not to stretch out.
She stood on my shoulder and I hoisted her up.
She was in the cave before me.
She was brave before me.
She was brave before I had to and this is important.

She clears the cave of snakes.
There isn't any wood.
There is rock, crumbled into dust.

The cave the color of
The color of what flows from my body when she touches it.
She says she won't let me in the cave.
She says she won't reach down and grab my hand and pull me up.
She says she wants to be alone, which is a statement.
A statement from the past.

In the past there were people.
There were crowds of people.
And people wanted to be alone.
People wanted to not be bothered because they spent most of their day running into people.
But now, we look out. And what we would give for another person.
For a person to walk by.
To walk by and say hello.

She puts her belly on the floor of the cave, steadying herself, grabs my hand, uses her knees to push her body back and I am in the cave too.

The surface is sand that has joined together.

That has become permanently joined together.

I lay on her and she supports me, there is nothing left to say but there is darkness.

It feels different.

It feels really different.

It's not about survival, it is about the moment before we pass through our body.

We are laughing as we run down the hill.

We are holding hands.

We kick up dust with our boots.

I crawl behind a rock.

She finds me.

The boulders are big and orange here. Where the boulders meet there is a crease. I nudge her into it, hips stabilized, unzip her pants, kiss her thigh as if it is the most fragile thing in the world, as if my lips could press into it and change it forever, like lips smashing into a pile of sand, she wants it so she pulls my face into her, I laugh because she wants it, because she wants it so so bad, I let her come, back arched against the rock: two nipples towards the sun, mouth agape.

We have no choice but to love each other. To make it work and to love each other.

Unclear what it was that brought us together. Unclear why we could not disconnect then it was just us.

Sand smells like something to protect yourself from. Sand smells like it should be close to water.

Sand here comes in each color: the red sand, the cream sand, the brown sand.

Sometimes she kisses me and she feels like someone else.

What called us was the desert.

We got in the hatchback and drove till the car overheated,

We drove and we drove, trying to get away.

Death was learned.
We put ourselves in bad positions.
Juniper pinyon pine.
What even grows anymore?

The white.
The white that comes off the coals.
When does it choose to be ash and when does it choose to be smoke?
We weren't responsible.
In our life.
I don't want to say in the time before because even now in this time I could be irresponsible.
I ate our last remaining pouch of nut butter.
I squeezed it out of the tube while she watched me.
She watched me and begged for a taste.
I said no.
I said this is mine.
I said never again will I taste almond butter and I wanted it.

Why does it always end this way?

What way?

The way where there are people left. Like a group of unrelated people is left and no one else is left and they don't know how it became this way.

But they all tried to survive.

Are we not trying to survive?

Every day there is a new horizon because the sand has moved.

We knew the wind at night came toward us because the
horizon grew closer.

From the top we see more sand.
More peaks, more bottoms.
We see light that looks like water.
Sand shows gravity like waves.
We gather a discarded piece of thick plastic.
She sits on the plastic, puts her legs in the air and slides.

God never knew the number of grains of sand.

When she reaches the bottom of the hill the plastic comes out
from under her and she falls, head in the sand, hair coiling
grains.

There were times when we barely existed.

When we slept at night and slept in the day.

There were times when our trail could be seen and times the wind covered it.

She is laughing at the bottom of the hill.

A big laugh.

I run down, tripping, falling, rolling till I reach her, roll into her.

She is laughing and she grabs my hand and rolls on top of me forcing my head into the sand. Sand makes clouds, makes haze, but doesn't make water. Her hand around my neck pressing me into the sand, I'm laughing, maybe she would prefer if I didn't laugh but I'm laughing and trying to find a breath, covering myself in her air.

Sand can continue to be sand or sand can become rock. Sand can become peak or sand can become valley. We stand on sand but it takes more energy than standing on rock. You can stand on sand but you won't be steady.

When she kisses me it's different. Her dry lips harden into shape and press against me.
This isn't desire. Desire is a goal.

Her tongue in my mouth, gritty. She presses into me till my hips hurt till my legs stiffen. Her binder flattens her chest and takes her breath. She pulls off her shorts, sticks her clit on my thigh and starts rubbing, her labia gets bigger and redder. Her smell on my thigh, quietly, her breath on my neck. I want to be tongued and I want her to rub. I want her to come on my thigh and I want to drip in her mouth. I want everything at the same time. She takes me, pulls my elastic shorts down and to the side, digs her tongue into me like all of her dehydration wants it, I try to create more and more wet for her and she sucks it. I want her to get deeper so I arch my back into a mountain, grabbing my ass to separate it, to make me bigger, to make me more open. She doesn't have to move because I am moving for her. I am falling with the wind, the wind that is her, the wind that is something we whisper at night to each other. I want her to stop because the feeling is too strong. She is pouring it into me. She won't stop. She refuses to stop. She pushes further and further and deeper and my circle clit flipped with her tounge and how how how is it. How does she how is she- I can't can't do anything but come and my back collapses into the sand the fall forcing her teeth into me.

Look into my eyes.

She looks into my eyes.

Why are you crying?

Because that felt like, that felt like...

A new challenge was an old challenge, how to be new to each other every day.

Thighs get big when I sit down. Rub against each other when I walk.

Beetle burrows into glittering sand.

A tree in the desert grows stout before it grows tall.

A smell in the desert, rarely stronger than the smell of sun.

Plants grow in the sand not down but across.

We knew it was time.

Time to leave the cave.
Go to the place of return. Of Visitors.

A circle.

Here in the desert rimmed with rocks.
The Vapors.
They were always waiting in the middle of the circle.
We cleared our nostrils, opened the package and inhaled as
quickly as we could.
Our sustenance, a fog.

When we sniff it our pores tighten, our stomach becomes per-
fectly full, our hair shines, a wave of energy spreads through our
veins.

She stops coughing.

That night in the city, her tank top, her baggy leather shorts. At the bar I take everyone. Dozens of first dates at the same table, wearing the same outfit, never to be seen again.

Why was it her who became an again? I am not sure. She says I was never sure.

She curves to fit the arc of the cave.
I lay myself in her.
There we are.
Two and rock makes three.
Her hands cannot avoid my thighs.
When she touches my thigh I don't know if it is
because she is holding me or if that hand is desire.
We were all wounded.
How to tell?
How to tell what she wants.
I hold her hand and press it into me.
She is big today.
And I?
Small.
Two legs bent and pressed together.
I open my legs a little.
Hope she will see.
There is enough room for her hand.
For her hand to slip right through.
Up and into.
Into and around.
Her hand, the dust, unavoidable.
Is she asleep?
Or is she thinking about where to put her hand?
Is she asleep or is she waiting to make me want it?
Is she asleep or is she wondering if I want it, afraid to move?
I turn my face to hers.

I wish I could remember how, but with her I always forget.
How, how to kiss her.
I turn my body.
My hand.
I reach out.
She is watching.
Watching the hand.
I scrape it across the dust collected in the cave.
Rubbing it into my skin.

Putting it up my nails.

You used to be up my nails
But now you're not.

I whisper so she can hear.
And then her hand is taking my shoulder.
And taking my mouth.
Filling my mouth.
A gasp from the hand constricting.
She pulls till I gag.
Her other hand laced with my hand pressing me into the floor
of the cave.
Her eyes on my eyes, big and brown.
She was born with 300 perfect lashes and I watch them curl,
unable to move.
Her body presses into my body and I feel the rocking.
Her hand unfurls against my clothes like a blossoming dick.
It moves like a dick, squirms like a dick, prods at me like a dick.
Trying to open me up I put my hand on her shoulder.
Push her to the ground.
I'm on top and she is mad.

I was trying to open you. I was trying to suck you.

But that's what I want. I want to be the one to do it.

I rip off her pants and shove my face between her legs before
she has time to react.
Filled.
Overflowing.
The wet from her body.
I want every mineral.
I want to lick up her dusted crack.
I want it now and I want it for a long time.
I have to pause because pleasure was coating me like wax.
Hand leans into her labia while my tongue is flipping over her

clit, moving it around.

I turn my face around her labia coating myself with her juice
breathing in deep and heavy.

I want you to want me.

I want you.

How can I know that?

Remember when we had jobs?
We had to work to survive.

The equivalence of work and life.

When the Visitors came down they told us they had the answer, the Vapors.
The answer to provision, to sustenance, without work.
Everyone said no.

They didn't want sustenance, they wanted to have more than their neighbor.
The competition was in every aspect of society, especially sex.
It led to violence.
Near the end we were so afraid of being hurt.
Near the end there was a party.
Everyone who was still around was dancing.
The drugs disappeared, no one could find them besides The Leaders.

I remember when you bought the powder from that tiny woman with the basket. Together in the basement of the club watching footage from the security cameras.
We went to your place on Putnam.
Your stairs always coated in dirt.
Your roommate away.
I'm on top of you.
I take your shirt off slowly in a way that shows I'm not fully confident.
I'm kissing you and holding your hip down.
My mouth into yours.
I lick my tongue around your lips forcing them open.
I get your tongue and press into it.
I feel my body enter the melted place, dripping into your body.
The moment I pause you take control wrapping your hand around my shoulder.
How could a hand so small control my whole body?
I try to shove you away to maintain control but you are stronger.
You force me to my back and I don't know when it happens but my pants are off.

Your hand is on me, not in, but on.
Before I can stop you, your tongue is on my clit.
Your tongue is a pleasure, then multiplied, multiplied by the highest multiplier.
You push into me further and further while grabbing my ass.
I can't tell if I am in the air or on the bed.
I can't tell if that is your tongue or your finger.
Sweat, every liquid.
The moment your tongue hit my clit I spoke in not language.
You are moving faster and faster it feels like every part of me is being pressed.
I don't want to come I try to nudge you away. But you need the taste of me
You need every bit to go down your throat and you suck and suck.
Engorged.
What is this place we have entered?
The language of tongue movement. I can't locate you.
I have lost direction.
Your tongue.
Your tongue.
My voice gets louder.
Your name appears in my head then dances away.
I'm squeezing my thighs together compressing your face and you look up at me and say
Now you are going to come
I say No No No No
which turns to yes
then yes yes
and your arms lengthen to hold my breast and my neck and my throat and my hip forcing me into the bed when I try to move.
I'm running my hand down you..
I push into your plush, the best feeling my hand has felt, your stomach, your breast, your cheek.
I rub my hand all over you to get you further into me.
I press your hand into me, you dent skin.
You pull my hair.

I lose vision.
Pleasure.
Pleasure.
A light.
Pleasure.
A lick.
Pleasure.
A drop of sweat down my tongue.
A lick of your ear and your neck till you groan.
Till I make you groan.
Do you like it?
I say or you say how could I know.
Tossing north then south then west.
Faster
Faster
Faster

Life was incoherent at best.
As in, at its best we embraced incoherence.

We grew more and more hairs.
Hairs dotting cheeks, hairs on our stomach. We were trees.

We never thought to track time passing because we were busy looking at sunrises, sunsets. Her sleep timed in order to witness both.

Did rocks wish to be dust?

What they necessitated as Politeness was actually just a way to control.

Sometimes bark looks like clay.
Sometimes we are shaped by something that isn't nature.

Time again for the Vapors.
Then after, time to reach a point called hunger.

6 million years ago there was a volcano here.
Even that I find hard to believe.
What is time after 100 years?
Time is so much bigger when you are in it.
Each spire is topped with a rock.
The rock protects the fragile sandstone below it.

The word last is used too much now.
Will this last will we last this is our very last _____.

Collecting grasses making sure they seem capable of cutting if only a little. Taking her wrist tying grasses around it. Then her thighs to her wrist, she's stuck in triangles. More and more grasses around arms and thighs pushing skin between the gaps in a place her grass turns red and drips. Her eyes unsure then closing. Spread her apart to the point where she could pop or the danger was breaking. She shakes the grass. It's not stronger than her. More grass. I need more grass.

I leave her stuck and opened for hours till the light turns.

I return to wake her.

Weaving grasses, her a basket.

The rock below her covered in sweat and blood. Then pleasure churns her and drips on rock.

If life means acquiring, did we die too?

We play a game.
What can I hold in my hand.
Her stomach.
Well, part of it.
Her breast.
Clumps of her hair.
Her knee.
We have to learn what is pleasurable again.

When I touch here?

Or here?

We don't have any of the tools we used to use: the double dildo,
the mask, the wax, the lubricant, the sheets, the mattress, the salt
lamp, the fishnet bodysuit.
Now we are just hands.
There is nothing to stop us but nothing to entice us.
No drink at the bar.
No attending the show.
No one to be jealous of.
Nothing to avoid.
The question of would we keep being together no longer
matters.
I don't need to convince her to be with me anymore.
We are just both here.
Always here.
What is desire without the challenge?
Or what is desire when time doesn't matter?
When all of your needs are met so quickly when the Vapors
arrive?

They used to repeat "First they come for _____ and if you say nothing, next they will come for you." And I wondered if they understood the real truth beneath that. That sentence is also saying that people only care when they are directly impacted. Which became true. But what if the other truth, the truth beneath it. What if instead it was "When they came for you, they were coming for me." Maybe that's what it was. Maybe that's why it all fell apart. No one understood that each part of them was part of another.

She has her legs hanging out of the cave.
Dangling.
Dangling to release the pressure.
It's almost like a chair.
A chair without a desk.
How many of us are there?
She thinks thousands, I think two.
The Visitors.
How many of them?

The air smells like dust and dries our noses.
I am kissing her hand.
She is telling me I have to always remember pleasure.

I always forget pleasure.

The day the Visitors first came we were together.

We were sitting down.
We were holding hands.
The restaurant makes you wear a bib but it doesn't cost extra.
She felt them first.
They spoke.
Right into her.
I was looking at her and I could tell it wasn't just in her head.
It was them and it was her.
Eyes jittering in a pattern I cannot predict.
Then the Visitors entered me.
When they first entered it was pearlescent.
They entered and I understood.
They told me it was the first message.
They would keep it short and give me time to think about it.
They would return for the answer on an undetermined
relatively soon date.
They told me I would have a choice.
I could choose to continue living the way I was living or I could
trust them.
The thought of trusting something I could not see was not
foreign to me.
Although the relations are obvious, most Christians didn't seem
to connect this entity to any sort of God.
Instead most identified the entrance as a sort of horror.
They did not see potential.
They did not see hope.
They wanted what had always been.
They wanted to continue their family line.

They had a lot of lines to keep.

The Visitors entered and left.
Before we spoke we knew our answer.
We knew we would trust.
We continued sucking the meat out of our crab legs.
And that was when a new word repeated: after.
We knew after that we would never be the same.
I stopped paying off my credit card, she stopped applying for jobs.
After.
In the before you could never know it was the before so you just lived your life.

To know, in this case, would also mean to be known.
We drag the whole bush out by small roots.
Carry it to the cave.
Set it on fire.
Our eyes burn from smell and smoke.
She is coughing, her eyes real big.
But the smell.
The bush on fire and that elegant smell.
The smoke, like slowly shaking wrists.

I tell her she isn't allowed to move and I start covering her limbs with rocks. First I choose the small round stones, the ones wind touched. I place them at her forearm her elbow her hand. I rub them in a little. Then I find the jagged ones and press them into her skin till she gets a little scared but nothing else. Soon her limbs are buried, pressure building on arms and pressure building below the belly in the place she hides. Stone on skin is only as soft as the skin and the gravity. She doesn't move as I walk   further and further for stones. A small stone fits in the hole at the hip of the underwear. A warm stone baked in heat at the place where thighs meet. A wet stone from the trickle that was a river at her lips and then dragged down her neck across her collar bone down the ribs. A long smooth stone I don't place anywhere at first. The sun says afternoon. Still hot as her sweat mixes with dust the brown darkens sweat from heat or sweat from what could happen sweat from strain of limbs held back from not being able to move for what seems like infinite time in this   position touching this dirt her stare following movement but what she sees is limited by the horizon of her own body. She looks at me and I look at her. I take the long smooth stone and press it through her underwear, her clit protruding like a salamander. I can feel her growing beneath my rock, her cloudy mineral builds till it darkens her underwear I'm barely moving the stone but she is moving her hips the only part of her she   really can move and I move her underwear till the stone is beneath it the stone warmed in sun and hands slowly slide it up her, her mouth opens and opens the rock moving from side to side like dust like something that isn't solid and I twist it in circles and I bend over to her and suck her clit out of her body lengthening it make it emerge making it grow bigger and bigger and I suck it like a gummy worm and she writhes and I don't move the rock it just fills her and her sweat becomes more mud and her wet becomes more mud and she remembers there is no one else and she lets herself make a sound then another sound then a scream but not one for help not one to be heard a scream because it bubbled into throat and has to escape if it doesn't escape if it doesn't exit if it doesn't escape the pressure of all

these little stones and they are all warm now they are all filled
with sun and they are holding her down and pushing it a bird in
the sky then another but I don't look up I only hear it and then
she rises further and further her clit touching everything
reaching out and not a word needed for any of it

At night we are not scared when the sky fills with stars.
All the lights out across the world so we find it again: darkness.

I can't even remember the last time. I undress her, it gets easier, her clothes unchanged for months. Memorizing buttons, snaps, zippers, folds. I know the clothes like I know her belly. Sometimes along the roads we find a shoe, a button down shirt, but not much. Most things crunchy covered in dirt and water. There is at once a lot of pressure being the few that remain and no pressure at all. If I could leave one thing it would be the energy in the space between my nose after she comes. She has an energy from somewhere. Energy tells her to run across the plateau. Energy tells her to lift rocks.

No matter where we are, the Visitors find us. We can sense the hours before they approach our own depletion. I'm moody and upset. I'm bloated. They arrive. We inhale the Vapors. We feel fine.

We walk.
We see in the distance a gathering of trees.
Fragrant.
Pine.
Dusted green, bark chipped.
Moving in the wind.
We haven't been there yet.
It's not even the end of our horizon.
Boots laced, every inch covered in dust.
Dust mixes with sweat.
Skin shines with earth.
The dust becomes clay, builds up in my creases.
I could be a statue.
My body could be hardened.
Chunks of it in my hair, I try to shake it out.
She looks at me, her mouth opens a little.
I try to see inside.
Mouth dripping and taut.
I want to see every inch of her tongue.
I want to know what it does when it's down on me.

The trees.
Our boots on.
We walk.
She says nothing.
But it's not quiet.
I feel myself getting big, filling with drip.
Thinking of the time before and the time before but when the
time is now and you're in it there is not any other time before.
As we walk my pants fill with my smell.
My smell mixes with pine, mixes with sun, mixes with dust.

I want you.

Not yet, not now.

We walk and walk and the air slightly dampens and we are
among the trees.
I throw her against a tree and bite her lip till she winces.

Not yet, not now.

She can hear it.
It's coming from there.
A gurgle.
A drip.
A hole in the rock.
She touches it, the water.
It's hot, hot and smelling of sulfur.
We move the rocks.
Create a circle.
Create a basin.
And the water pools up.
She lifts bigger and bigger rocks.
I stare.
Her bulging arm.
Building.
She digs with her hand till she reaches the clay.
Building up the tub, brown water splashing.
I lick it off her forehead, it grits my tongue.
Swallow.
Steam is coming off the pool.
The noise.
Her button.
Opened.
Laces popped off boots.
Socks hang on the rock.
Feet first squish into mud then the mud settles and it's water.
Piece by piece she puts her body in it.
Pubic hair mounds up, makes a tower.
I watch her nipples cloud with steam.
Her body feels like mud when I touch it.
I wrap my legs around her hip.

Press my pubic bone into her thigh.
I move back and forth till my clit touches her thigh.
Rubbing.
She grabs my hip and shoves me down onto her again and
again.
Breasts bounce, the water splashes on my face.
The smell of mineral and sweat and cunt.
I grab her neck and push my whole body into hers.
Not worrying about bruises.
As I smack my clit on her face her eyes roll back.
Held by water and mud.
Again and again.
When the body hits the other body the feeling is pleasure.
Pleasure that eats away.
Pleasure that decays any sort of thought.
Hand.
Hand reaches my clit, shakes it.
Shakes it hard.
The grit.
Moving around.
The warmth.
Holding.
Holding hand.
Holding ass.
Body against body.
And finally she lets a little sound leave her lips.
She wants it.
In the same rhythm as me.
Breast into breast.
My hand charges her clit.
We shake each other.
Her teeth reach into my neck and I cannot be contained.
I collapse into her.
Then she into me.
A whimper.
From my lips.
A whimper.

Energy exits our bodies like steam.
We don't move for an hour.
Till the water pools to our necks.
The sun tricks us and begins to fall.
I only put my boots on.

We walk out of the forest.
Steam trickles out our pores.
Drips fall to the forest floor.
Our mineral, our spread.
Hands held.
The darkness arrives and even that air feels filled with moisture.

What did I really want?

We sit in the cave and the air changes.

We look out and the clouds drift in faster than walking. They darken and descend. From where we sit we can see the first drop then the second then the pour. New little rivers sift dirt taking smaller particles further. A snake caught in the rain tries to move before being taken away. I want to lick every drop from every branch.

Before the water there is a sign. Water churns up silt, air. Particle turns to foam like the dessert you never wanted. To the west we see it trickle between a plant that stretches across the ground like fingers and one that rises up like horns. The foam seeps down newly made ridges. Reluctant at first then compounding into river then compounding into flood.

From our cave we are safe but so much isn't. Short rooted cacti is unhooked from the dirt and falls. Agave flowers four feet high with the thinnest stems. So much was learned over so much time. Like how to cut the stem of the tall flower, squeeze the innards, ferment it, make alcohol. Alcohol from plant stems and we never thought about it each night in the city in the dark.

Water making mud then stopping the air smelling like everything underneath. I desire her in this place where everything dies. I desire her in the cave as we watch the flood that could have killed us. I desire her because it doesn't matter if we die as long as we die at the same time. No sound but drips. Before the flood when it was just rain every bug came out to swarm the air like they heard if they didn't they would die, the air filled with erratic specks.

Chest growing & lengthening, everything becoming strong. We have been together so long I can see it changing and I always thought this would end desire but desire is never ending just a series of unfolding shells a shell in a shell and when you think there is no shell there is one even tinier to open up.

I am unknowable. I have become unknowable. I don't have much left to say so I don't say it. I hold onto it like I hold onto her. I can't let it go ever for anything. I watch her eyes trace the path of water stream and I block her field of vision I put my chest in her face and she has no choice but suffocate and suffocate as elation as in light headed as in we create warmth and we move together quickly then slowly so much pressure built up inside, so much witnessed, I could come in a minute or never at all. It feels like the pace could never be maintained it feels like if I don't do something she won't love me anymore it feels like I have to control it because fate stopped working. It feels like hand in her pants squeezing her big clit between my fingers squeezing her like the cleaned flesh of a cactus. Licking her like I need the water watching her chest tighten.

The Vapors make her breasts become smaller and smaller; now they held her chest tightly offering no bounce at all. Her hardened nipple enveloped by my hand and I lick it I tell her I am rain I tell her I will drip on everything and I part her labia put in a finger pull it out, lick it a long lick all through my throat she tastes like mud and vinegar a scent I'll never remember so I keep having to get more of it her hip bruising my thigh hands in her hands around her hands across her hand now not enough needs warm wet tongue so I lick it slow but fast now slow for no time and then fast fast and I suck it so she can hear it so she hears it go in and out of my mouth she has learned to moan here in the desert where no one can hear her before she never said anything at all but now a moan in my ear then she grabs my face and shoves it into her clit, till she hears me pant and I hold her thighs apart so my face won't be crushed and she wants more and more and a pain in my neck, I ignore, a pain in my side, I ignore, I only feel the small breath I must take and she tries to enter my mouth whole as if she could fold in that way and be lost inside me as if she could move and the pleasure is too big it knocks me over onto the rock floor and she shudders on top of me, our warmth consumed by rock.

Something about my finger in her lingers.
Is it peppery milk?

Sticky and changing.

Each day a different taste.

I shoot my finger into her labia.

People always put
Unconditional with Love.

We didn't believe in that.
We believed in conditional love.
We wanted our love to be conditional.

We wanted to be free to leave, to be free to stop loving.
In the time before, the people who birthed us used the word
Love.
They hurt us and said it was because they loved us.
I didn't call it love, I called it hurt.

Watching myself in their eyes, seeing their frown.
In the time before these people who said they loved us sought to
control our movements.
They tracked where we were.
I called it pain.
Maggots.
They looked like maggots.

On the rock I spread my legs they fall off either side expanding my open exhale, smell the earth around me, the sun is out today the dirt is heating up emitting dust emitting smell I'm alone for once and I inhale the sun hitting me I pull down elastic I'm alone surrounded by rocks surrounded by air and sun and dryness thinking of myself and everything I have done thinking of myself and what I carry thinking of the places I've chosen and how my ass squishes into the rocks thinking of my creases filled with dirt and no way out here to be clean or to maintain puffs of hair everywhere my wet smell mixes with dry air nothing but me and earth earth   me on earth   earth in me   earth on me curl my fingers around the rock feel my nails try to dig in feel the rock rejecting my nails making my hands hurt a hand on my clit up and down not in, up and down my hips move to receive me my hips want it more than anything my hips into my hand.

What is giving to someone who never asked?
How can they even receive it?

No one is around anymore.
No one needs to know what we have.
No one needs to know what we make together.
We thought it would be a sort of freedom but-

We walk towards what we can feel.
We walk towards where the Visitors go.
We arrive early.
The sun in the air.
The dirt in the air.
The animals are walking around.
The lizard on the rock.
Everyone waiting for the Vapors.
I fall asleep on her shoulder as we wait.
Then the energy shifts, wakes me.
The Vapors are placed.
We open the package.
Breathe the vapors in.
I kiss her, refreshed.

It's not a shower but it's something.

You don't need a shower, you would lose all your smells.

I don't know if it is the stress or what but I haven't bled in
months.

I feel like I haven't bled in years.

We walk back to our cave quietly.
We don't want to wake anyone.
We are used to being quiet.
We are used to the city.
The city is so loud but demands so much quiet from everyone.
She kisses the back of my neck where the sweat concentrates.

I don't know what I wanted.

I forget what I wanted.
I wanted to be known.
The only way I could figure out how to be known was to give
other people everything.

The air tonight sings a song like a hiss.
It flows past the hole of the cave making us feel like we are the
insides of pipes.
We let the plants do whatever they want.

Collecting smells at dusk.
The bush has to be sage.
The stringiest sage.
We didn't bring our knife.
As we tear it we see the bark is composed of condensed strands.
But then where do the rings come from when sliced?
I collect bark from the ground.
How to describe a smell when every smell here is dirt and
something?
Bark crumbles in my hands, turns to dust, coats me in smell.
We are trying to create something.
This is our doing for the day.
This is what we choose to do.
Another bush.
Leaves like waxen furls.
When crushed in my hand smells like green and grass.
We collect reeds and leaves and pieces of growth.
Our arms are full: bushels.
We bring it into the cave.
She lights the fire.
One by one we throw it in.
We track the changes in smell.
We agree the sage is the best but it could be tied to a memory.
Everything else is new and fills our noses, goes up to our brain.
Fills us with lightness and again we laugh.
We didn't think so many new experiences could be our life.

We were used to repetition.
We still repeat.
Nothing feels the same.

I wake up and my jaw is sore.
The sleep.
The second sleep.
We wake up.
Then we fall asleep again.

Because we can.
Because we don't need to be anywhere else.
I turn over.
Her cheek, the perfect dark brown dots.
I couldn't be a better lover if I tried.

As in, I don't know how to be a better lover.
As in, I always get in the way.
As in, we have been through too much to really forget.
As in, I'm trying.

I try then I get angry.
She wakes up not saying much and hops out of the cave.
I watch her gathering rocks,
making patterns in the dirt.
She laughs when they look like petroglyphs.
She laughs because we have created and destroyed every
technology and are back to petroglyphs.
I'm angry she didn't invite me.
The anger is stupid, but controls me.
I can't find a way to ask it a question.

When our bodies change we have had the Vapors more times than I remember.

She starts climbing up and down rocks to have something to do. My back elongates, doesn't grow, just stands up straight. An era of posture formed by shame. One day I wake after sleeping on the rock and each notch of spine ticks into place and I'm standing up, pressure off my hips, pressure off the balls of my feet. I can fill my lungs with breath. Eventually my shoulders too roll back. I become the shape I was intended.

The last thing to change is clitoris. Before it pressed against her body, now it pokes itself out. I can suck it out, flip it with my finger, now there is a left side a right side a side stuck to the body and a side that leaves what is this dream what is this her that changes the more I know it

what is never stagnant I'm reminded of
the ways before I was taught to think
solidity when it really was movement I
wonder if this is why we remain because
we knew it before because we wanted it
before I wonder how to keep changing
and how easy it was the Visitors taught
us what they already knew: your body
could become whatever you wanted
and then after could become the next
thing you wanted it seemed so clear now
so obvious

unlearn forget mourn forget
what we wanted to forget what
we couldn't forget what we
had to forget to survive that is

called mourning a
recognized forgetting a
forgetting that starts in the
throat and moves throughout
mourning becomes ritual then
mourning becomes forgotten
the only way to mourn forever
was to never forget and most
people tried to forget as soon as
possible most people got three
days off of work maximum and
then they returned and no one
asked where they were or what
they were doing
forgetting already forgetting
again and again forgetting
where you were born or how
you left that place forgetting
your firsts and forgetting the
hands you didn't want
forgetting little touches and
big touches all of us forgetting
everything forgetting it again
and again we forgot it so many
times we didn't know how to
remember and sometimes we
danced and sometimes we
celebrated but I felt uneasy in
every mode I felt like every
mode I was acting and I was
exhausted from every role,
families gathered and I felt
exhausted holidays celebrated
and I felt exhausted who was
the inventor of it of that and
why   I was expected to do so
much and sometimes I forgot

to do what I was told to do like
taxes

each thought a river the more
the Vapors changed her body
the more I wanted it

the more her body became her
the more I wanted it

What survives? What do we leave behind?

Our car ran out of gas months ago.

We walk. We need a new setting. Something else to look at, a different view out of a different cave.

We walk for miles and days until more green. Ponderosa pine, bristlecone pine, juniper, white fir. We come across an abandoned park and take the remaining pamphlets.

They give us these names for plants. They tell us how to get to the dwellings.

Before we were here there was always someone else. There were other people creating other lives. Creating movement in rocks, creating their own sort of permanence. Only unreadable files. The trash left at the park is what future will see first. They will see that people drove distances to look at remnants of other peoples, people they destroyed. They thought the destroyed lives were so simple, so mysterious, and they didn't remember why they don't exist anymore.

An hour more of hiking and we turn a corner. There built into the rhyolite are walls, walls with windows and ladders. Each stone chiseled from the rock, stacked, and glued with mud. The walls of the structure look like the walls of the cave. The ceiling of the cave, black. Fire had been here. The doors, shaped like bodies with outstretched arms, have to be climbed into.

She pulls me up into it and we look at the mesa across the river. As soon as we sit, it begins to rain. First drops small then they begin to pound. Water creates lines down cliffsides. She holds my waist and we stare out into it. Water flattening color. Water the only noise now. Years of witnessing this rain. Rain creating pause then creating moment after rain when everything wakes up again.

While it rains we begin to count the rooms, 46. Small and large, square and circle. This was built around people, shaped like their hands. This was built to be close to other people. Enough rooms for enough people. Graffiti scratched in some walls. People saying they were here to the people before and the people after.

Rain stops. Heat creates steam. Vapor rising smelling like mud and pine. We decide to stay for a while to learn as much as we can piece together. These too were people who vanished. They only left how they dwelled.

We pick a room to sleep in and kick out the rocks. Her hand reaches out and I lick the dust off her fingers. How many miles have we walked and how many miles could we go? Her hand tastes like calcium carbonate, phosphorus.

Again we walk till the ground
becomes flat as in the hills are
hills and not mountains,
as in I forget what pain is like,
as in my legs do not tire,
as in I could walk all day,
as in her and me.

I love you for now & now is all we have.

Here in the flatland the dust drifts forever.
There is no end anywhere.
There are trees.
The bottoms rough.
The leaves blade out.
Struggle to emerge.

When we lay on the ground these trees break our horizon.

A name was a place.
A place was somewhere.
Was supposed to be different.
From the other places.

How much we forgot
when we were trying
to get somewhere.

When we were trying
to survive.

I'm not even sure if I want to survive.

I am here. She is here.
A thing we repeat.
I wanted to know
how to be with her,
but I only knew the performance.
I knew so well how to sleep it off.

Here in the flat land there is no cave.

We find somewhere else to sleep.

She weaves together fronds.
Forms a blanket.
Kicks the rocks from the ground.
Makes the ground smooth.
The sky mellows then pastels.
Then the light is gone.
Then the moon is gone.
Nothing but stars.
Stars clump, make belts.
Stars flicker, then extinguish.

Eight minutes and twenty seconds is all the time we would have
of a dead sun and us not knowing.

She grabs my hand, kisses it.
To our right a tree obscures a constellation.

I'm afraid of not knowing when to leave.

All the years I could have left you, all the moments I wanted to
leave you.

I was used to leaving, I decided to try something new.
I was used to leaving and I wanted to stay.

If I said how many shooting stars crossed over us you wouldn't believe it. As in, it would be too perfect of an image.

The smell of blood used to arrive monthly but stopped. The Visitors told us we didn't need it anymore and made it stop. My stomach poofed out. They got better at finding us and we got better at finding them. Figured out which rock formations they like, what numbers of stones they prefer. We never see them arrive, we just feel them. Feel them all in our body like being a teen and feeling god. They were here. We reach for the package. Open the Vapors. Inhale. Filling us then releasing us. They know what we want. They bring us closer to them, holding us with their air. We first thought we were their experiments but now we feel more and more like their children. They tell us which direction we have never been before and again we walk. Our bodies relaxed and tightened. The Vapors release any stiffness. As quickly as they arrived they are gone, until we need them again.

They tell us we can live as long as we would like and then we can die.
They tell us when we die that energy will be recycled.
In that way we will continue.
They tell us what we experienced our whole lives wasn't fit for any being.
They tell us we are opening up the earth.
They tell us we are free in life and free in death.
They tell us this wasn't true before.
They tell us they are proud of us and when they say this we are not their children.
When they say this we are them.

We wake on the blanket she weaved.
Sand was supportive enough.
So much is a memory now.
Gold leaves, ginkgo seed popping.
My finger around her neck, desire never stopping.
Desire, release, desire, release.
Room for movement, no room for movement.
Happiness, an unknown emotion.
Happiness, an invented emotion.

I use my hand to rub my clit clit throbs through I come fast
I know I'll come again my face between her legs sucking her
elongated clit mouth filling and filling then tossed. She puts her
clit inside me in and out and in and I take her between my legs
telling her more more.

She says she's thinking of the way my hip feels to be held, the way my thigh feels to be held, the way my arm feels to be held, softness comes endless.

She says I was thinking how desire multiplies, how it moves. I was thinking about my new clit, the foreskin I grew, the way your tongue tries to push in it, the way you dust.

She says Why can't you just be happy they are sustaining us? Isn't this what you wanted? No work, no money, a life that is all time.

She runs down the hill breaking dry dirt into dust. She finds a ledge, throws herself off it. She tries to break her body.

I scream at her. She runs further away. I can't get to her, she walks through the brush, her skin bleeds.

I fall to the ground. The callousness. She's trying to die before me. She's trying to leave me alone with all this time.

Even here I'm not enough.

It darkens and she doesn't return. The moon full lights enough so I wont trip on an animal. I go towards the cliffs. I look down and see her body, blood dripping. I find a path to get to the bottom and crawl down it, twigs and rocks cutting my skin. I reach her body, she doesn't move. I throw a rock at her, I kick her, she doesn't move.

You can't die before I do.

I beg the Visitors to send the Vapors, to come down and heal her broken back, to wake her up.

I don't know how to reach them but I repeat the desire hoping they have access to my mind or my sound. Then three lights float down. Metal sphere. I unlock the package, pull out the Vapors, I put them to her nose, let them float up into her.

Her skin hydrates, I pinch it, it falls again, supple.

She opens her eyes, speaks. Her voice hasn't changed. No one would know she had just tried to die.

They didn't let me die... the Visitors wont let me die.

It wasn't them. It was me. I asked for them.

Why didn't you let me die?

You're selfish.

You saving me is selfish. You just don't want to be alone.

She cries, not connected to any one thing, but years of all the things. Years of not getting to choose anything. Years of wanting to die. Years of feeling alone. Years of her power taken from her.

I hold her, enclosing her with me, a cocoon. She falls asleep inside of me. Wakes. We decide for now to live until we don't want to live any more.

We decide to walk.

I didn't care if she wanted me because I wanted myself
wherever we decided to stop walking I could pour rocks into
my pussy let it grate draw blood lick blood reaching my arm
further down my throat wanting to shit out every end.

She said dust to dust. I said that's cliche. She said it was what she wanted. She wanted me to be dust. She brushed my skin. She pulled at my skin with her teeth. She pulled skin off me, pain coming down wet on my face. She placed the skin on a rock. Let the sun heat it up, dry it out. She crumbled it between her fingers. She spread this dust on my skin like paint then licked it. She made me sit in the sun till I peeled. Slowly she pulled sheets off me mixing it with my other dusts. She said dust to dust as in dust join other dust as in dust is all we have as in dust is all of us as in dust was all we created before we left as in dust is not debris dust is what remains. She grabs my dust with her tongue. She dries me out with her desire. I wanted to be dry. I wanted to thirst.

A crevice. In a crevice. Mounds separate. She wraps strips of grasses around my head. Separates the strands where they meet my eyes. She takes leaves from a yucca plant. Takes a stone pounds the leaf separating the fiber from the pulp. She flips the leaf pounds and pounds. I am still and standing. She scrapes the leaf till it looks like stiff green hair. Pulls strands and begins to twist. Twist and roll and pinch. Strands strengthen become braid. Two feet of rope she connects fibers and braids. She pulls the rope hard, it does not break. She slips part of the cord between my wrists wraps it ties it making a leash from my hands to hers. She pulls at the rope until I have no choice but to move. The fibers begin to cut into my skin, thinner than needles. Green rope dripped in the red that beads on my skin. She takes me in silence across the dirt. She tells me to close my eyes. Cups her hand in the dirt and spits on it making mud and covers my eyelids in it. A heavy sinking keeps my lids down. A pause then she begins to walk, wrapping the rope around me and something. She pulls the rope tight then I feel it, cactus. My back is cut with needles, hundreds of needles. She massages me into it. Pushes my stomach till my back arches out. Then she moves pressure into my hips, needles reaching toward asshole. Her hands a rhythmic kneading, points full for pressure. Pain, a familiar feeling made unfamiliar. Pain becomes desire in her hands.

I hear her walk away and walk until I can't hear her anymore. The mud on my eyes dries, feels permanent. I hear wind across the dirt, a crow in the sky. Stagnant air on my body. I drip. Blood and sweat pooling in my shoes. Sun on top of my head. Hours till darkness and where is she. I think I hear footsteps but they don't come near. My unopened eyes push me into boredom which pushes me into sleep.

I wake to pain at my neck, her smell in the air. Pain shifts from behind me to in front of me, all over me. She strokes my neck then my collar bone with a piece of cactus leaving trails of red. . The pain dizzying till my mind escapes to a soft place. She senses this and begins to hit me, needles sinking into skin and dragging. Skin separates blood pours or is it sweat or is it blood. Smell of iron and salt. She increases speed till I become numb and cannot stand. I let go of control of my body, drooping, held only by rope. She pauses. I hear the cactus she holds drop. A sudden warmth, tongue on neck. She cleans the blood from my body. She uses her teeth to cut the rope and I fall on top of her. A word, what is the word, is it drained? Or is it letting? To drip I must have created it. Hours later I wake. Touching my eyes the mud crumbles off into my hand. Open my eyes. See her, covered in me.

We walk.

We arrive at the canyon as the sun is setting. A couple of cars are still parked in the lot. As we walk towards the entrance to the park trail I see trash cans. Metal ones. Filled with holes. The wind blowing what remains: coffee cups, chip bags, napkins. I put my head down in it to remember what that smelled like. Smell leaves before anything. Coffee smells like rain and earth and burnt bread. Feels odd to walk on pavement after so much sand, so much dirt. It's so easy to walk on concrete. It is so easy when the trail is decided for you. I wondered what this was like with people. When the trail straightens again we lose our balance. A canyon of this size has its own gravity. It tries to suck us in. It dares us to jump off the ledge. Dares us to get closer. I wrap my fingers around the fence. The fence isn't high enough to prevent anything. If I close my eyes I can hear the canyon, birds flying. An occasional screech from an animal. Rock changes color the further down you go. Earth breaks itself open. What can we rely on? Earth cracking, ground moving.

I want to scream down the canyon but I can't find my voice. She screams and it is immediately eaten up by the canyon.

Red rock yellow rock brown rock black rock.

How many more days do we have?

She told me tenderness meant pain as in that tender spot on her knee from before.

Words say very little anymore. Words mean almost nothing. A word from her spills maybe once a day. Not much to talk about.

We talk about beauty. We talk about weather. We talk about wind. We talk about mourning. We talk about who we left. We talk about forever. We talk about the other people we would date instead if there were other people. Out here I see no pain. Nothing has broken. Nothing has been demanded. I didn't have to sell anything to pay my rent. I no longer have to suffer. I was so used to suffering. What is life if I am not suffering? If I am not in pain? Without pain I feel like something is missing.

Before, the government decided what had the most beauty and protected it. Paved roads to arrive on, trails to hike on, shops to buy from. Small towns sprung up around the most beauty. Trash piling up outside the town, gas stations, empty pouches of beef jerky. Land protected meant something similar to what they called protective as in father protects daughter. It isn't like don't go here, it's like We Control It. Each place of beauty had a commemorative stamp. Collect all the stamps and you have collected all of the stamps.

She's somewhere around leaning against a tree spacing out. Too much time in the day. I'm afraid to be present because there is too much time in the day. If I was present for all of the time in the day I would be doing exactly what I am doing right now: crying. I wouldn't be able to keep walking down the government paved roads. I would be crying. I would probably begin to think about the form of government we survived. The kind that stole land then paved roads to reach it and then created an environment for only certain people to visit. Government killed everyone to ensure the beautiful place would never be too crowded.

It was solidity, her solidity. Consume the Vapor watch the hips flatten, posture change, belly pulled in. Each fog a little bit of energy a little fluid a little in the thigh a little then a little bit more. When she walked through the sand she never faltered. Her feet surprisingly small emerging from legs just poking out she had none of my limbs as in length as in my limbs were too stretched out.

Somehow I always thought I was smaller than I was. Always surprised when my head hit a branch or my leg swiped a cactus.

She always knew exactly where she was. Her body didn't make mistakes. Her fingers landed exactly where she planned. I never saw her trip on anything and all we did was walk. I observing her, she observing the land I led us through and thus observing me by observing the land I chose to cross. Knowing body because it is moving through across against. She was never wind she was always rock. Seeing her in tattered underwear taking a break from pants from a button at the stomach. She looked so small in her underwear but so big in real life. She didn't look like any gender when we were walking but when she was standing there in underwear beneath the tree with spikes she looked like girl.

The lies, unfurled. Floated around us. Emerging. The lie of what we wanted. The lie of how to be together. The lie that held so many together for so long wasn't enough anymore. The lie wasn't that we needed each other because we needed each other, we needed everyone. The lie began and kept unfurling. The lie of who I was, the lie of who she was. The lie of solidity in relationships. We were moving too much in what direction? Relationships invented to achieve a sort of stability. Now, everything lost, is this the ultimate instability or the ultimate stability?

Her body. Unwrapping. The damage I wanted to do to it. The way I wanted to hold her while she cried. The way dust cracked across her skin. We were each unfolding each other looking for a sort of core that wasn't there.

Seeking. Seeking. Desiring. Possessing. Oh, it was in the possessing.

We had possessed each other, in public, in private. If I showed enough care then maybe finally it would return to me.

The cactus gets bigger and bigger. Thorns poke out.

I could say something about the protective urge but nothing will protect us here or anywhere.

Nothing will protect us and we will hurt. Thorn in her arm and it comes out red. Thorn pierced through her lip then her nose. Red dripping.

She doesn't speak. She waits for me to move.

She sits.

I cut the cactus down the middle. It splits.

I cut it into a strip, place the flesh on my hand making a glove of thorns, lean it towards her, a gentle prick, she shudders, she leans, she moves away. The thought of hurt charges the spikes like a magnet and she is repelled.

Dust coating our arms, our throats, Dust in our teeth and our ears. Dust everywhere.

Cactus falls over, decays, dries up, leaves skeleton. Cactus skeleton, a pile of long slender sticks. We pick them up run around churning up dust. We try to joust we try to hit each other, laughing, skeleton sticks snap on my belly and I fall over. She laughs, I laugh.

To create a feeling of future we try almost death. Pain has opened us up. Pain has made us all body, all dust.

I forget the names for things but I can still describe it. One looks like a rock but when you press into it you know it's alive. Waiting for water. Everything here waiting for water.

Long sticks of green from the dirt like a pack of carrots.

I try to keep track of what I have seen and what I haven't seen but without a name it becomes the same.

Cut open the leaf, press out the jelly, wrap her in it, catch a wind, moment of cooling, feel wind further, our skin coated in jelly stuck with dirt, I lick it off her arm, grit in my teeth, dirt in my mouth, her arm, taste of her arm, and I want her chest, taste of her chest, and I want her stomach, taste of her stomach, and I want my whole hand in her throat. She chokes on it spits me out we slide towards each other again. Jelly sticks and makes us attach, skin stretched out, she looks like god and smells like earth. My hands pushing away at her unwrapping her taking her in my hand, taste everything have to taste everything taste her sour and her gold, my spit drips down her chest, and I don't stop licking, her hand goes down to her clit, her jelly hand her dirt hand grit hand rub a little more friction than usual turns her tender, and she rubs, closes her eyes, mouth making little circle, she rubs and rubs, warmer and warmer, warmer and warmer. Tremble. Then falls. Energy sucked, my tongue, her hand, I sit on her chest with my ass in her face she takes it, spreads it apart, her tongue her tongue in me her tongue her tongue outside then inside outside, I'm trembling now I'm dizzy, she pulls me further into her mouth her mouth licking all of me at once clit to asshole she sucks me in pulls me further and further out out stretch skin stretch asshole stretch labia and I try to focus try to take my tongue and put it in her try to lick her like she licks me and we are a circle of sucking and blowing and coughing and her her her taste like taste like fermented earth and tastes like her and her calves in the dirt, she shakes, I quiver, I open I drain in her mouth, she gasps, I scream across the valley her throat opens her noises her hands can't even hold me she's crying to someone the someone that is pleasure the someone in her body.

Uses a flat rock, digs out earth, lowers her head into the ground, closes her eyes, I cover her head in dirt so she cannot open her eyes, a hole for the nose, no hole for the mouth. Sounds don't reach her ears. She cannot know where I am. I walk away. A direction. I see the sun shift, I return to her. Arms and legs out. I kiss her thigh and she moves in surprise. She doesn't know how long I left her, I do not know how long I left her. Every time I leave her the possibility, the possibility of never finding her again. I try to leave in straight lines but hills make them curve. I pull her shorts to her ankles. Her clit falls down into her labia, forces it open, I take it in my mouth, sucking in and out, it grows, it winds around my tongue, it has a life of its own it moves with no regard for me. Her thighs shake, I hear her swallow a moan. If she opens her mouth it fills with dirt and all she wants is to open her mouth, open her eyes, open anything. I feel her move, I feel her sticky wave, I know her rhythm. I know her body. I know her body more than mine because I can see it from every angle. I know her small hips, her arm muscle, her tooth that overlaps the other tooth, the crease in her skin, the dots on her cheeks, the arch of her toe, the tightness of her breasts pulled against her chest. I know she wants to come so I walk away. I walk till she is as small as my finger, her agitation, palpable, her desire to scream, her want. Her want. Her want dripping into the ground and floating in the air. I laugh at how much desire she has, how much she wants me. I laugh and I don't give her what she wants.

Cutting pieces of white cactus flesh, chewing on it, puking.

Everything changed. We left each other.

Are you happy?

No. Not at all.

How long have you been unhappy?

Unhappy? Always. Unhappy with you? I don't know.

Why didn't you say something?

We were trying to survive. We were always just trying to survive. I couldn't see in front of me at all. And you were always there. Maybe it was nice for you to always be there.

You just never thought about leaving?

No.

But were you happy?

No.

Sometimes it feels like happiness is too much to ask for. Too much pressure for any relationship. I'm not happy but maybe happiness isn't what I wanted. I wanted to be with you. I wanted to fuck you, open you up, pour my hands in you. I wanted to tear you apart, make you bleed, lick it with my tongue. I didn't want you to be with anyone else. Ever. I mean you can fuck whomever but I wanted everyone to know at the end if was you and me.

And now no one remains. So what's the point?

You want to unravel? You want to be in the desert by yourself? Wandering till you fucking die?

Maybe it would be a nice change of pace. I could disappear. I wouldn't have to think about you worrying about me because you wouldn't be allowed to worry about me because we wouldn't be together.

If that's what you want, leave. We both don't want each other. I'm sick of your smell, your wandering, your silence. I'm sick of wanting more from you and never getting it. I'm sick of your lies and the way you stare at the sky.

If we find each other again we can talk about it.

We turned around. Walked away from each other till even the crunchy footsteps could not be heard. Our tracks were covered in wind. We could not be found and we could not find. There was nothing to hold us together and nothing to bring us back.

All feelings felt their opposite when I knew I was completely alone. When I knew for a fact I would die alone.

I collect twigs and bend them till they crack. Rigid lines in the wood.

I pierce my skin in a pattern. Spell PAIN then laugh because I tried to turn my pain to suffering but pain was just pain.

I make cuts around my breasts, try to leak them out, get them off my chest.

Her hairs will grow across her stomach and no one will be there to lick them. To twist them around their tongue.

The sustenance is so abundant now that animals probably won't even bother to eat my meat.

Fill my mouth with dust. Wet dust warm dust mouth dust. Cannot speak will not speak mouth of dust feeling dust tasting dust taste of dust is everything but dust it is whatever fell off into the sand piss plant whatever. I try to carry some in my throat but I choke and it comes out. When I say it I do not mean all of it. No. absolutely no no no my mouth remains coated a thin film no not that it is coated like a glaze like a glaze on a fucking cake. My life, this is my life. Heartbroken. Alone. Surrounded by dust. Hopeless doesn't mean anything anymore. She left me with nothing. We chose together to end apart. We chose to come here and couldn't make it work. We chose to be together and couldn't make it work. There is no one else to go to, no one else to fuck. It is air, it is dirt, it is land so much land.

What made desire in the first place? Desire created from what everyone called lack. The more I walk the more I know I contain everything. I lack nothing, I am anger I am silence I am scream I am fist fucking myself. Why did they tell us about lack when they should have told us about grief?

Grief was everywhere and here too in everything. Grief in the dried up river bed. In the abandoned bodies, the rotting bodies, the bodies that no longer move. The bodies of everything and everyone. I want juice to drip down my face and I don't want it to be my own.

How many days pass, what is time when no one is keeping track? What was time ever at all? If time passes and nothing changes, was time ever passing?

I feel cold on my body. Shiver. Start looking. Not just wandering, I'm looking. There must be a cave. Another cave. Rocks grow out the ground. Wind hits the rock. The cave. The water freezes cracks open makes a cave. Water stronger than rock water stronger than rock and it could kill me if it came here. If all the water gathered and came to me. Built and built, pushed me against the rock, I'd be dead.

The cave first looks like a spot of dark rock then as you get closer you can see the air push itself into the rock, you can see texture and depth. Maybe not a perfect cave, but a cave. The air changes. From the cave I begin to see it. Dust gathers. Thickens. Wisps at the top. Across the valley gathering bigger. Looks slow as it comes toward me but when it hits the mouth of the cave it's nothing but speed. I unbutton my shirt, stick my chest out of the cave. Churned up dust hits my chest, warming it with friction till it burns. I don't move. It peels my skin back. Feeling. I had wished for feeling.

When the dust storm settles the sun returns. The ground looks all churned up like a giant sneeze passed through. Leaves me so alone. In the distance the color of the storm changes because the color of the land changes. What is cloud and what is dust?

Now the only way to tell time is land. The seasons of dirt on my shoes. My feet calloused over. To be desired again was what I wanted. Where is she? How did she experience the storm? Did she find her own cave? Did she lay on the ground and let it take her?

To be apart made missing her possible.

Screaming in the cave. Screaming outside of the cave. Screaming. Screaming. How to end this. How to end this.

I know it has been months since her hair in my face. I don't know if she is missing me. I don't even know if I miss her or I miss the me that is seen.

It's time for sustenance so I walk until I arrive. The animals are here too. Their faces filled with boredom. When it floats to me I grab my vapor in my hand, suck it through my nostrils. The vapor tingles in my nose feels like salt. The vapor travels through me again. But now my needs are different. Without her. I feel the vapor travel between my legs, open up my body, tingle my clit. I fall to the ground. Try to steady myself. Try to sink into the earth. Vapor tingle vapor toss. My eyes roll back. The pleasure, confusing, but pleasure. I feel myself growing I heaten I tense I toss my head into the rock my legs shake my hands sweat my stomach turns my lungs fill I tell myself to breathe I force myself to breathe the vapors wave across my clit practicing. They learn everything, I worry. They aren't her but they take her form, a thick tongue. A tongue that is air or cloud. Come closer make me feel like I am held. I want to be held held held again and held and I want to be with her I want her again is it the closeness to her but the not her the almost her the conjured her my head hits the rock my vision leaves I'm being tossed I'm being turned I'm being opened they are opening me they are floating in me they are bouncing little balls on my insides they are every feeling at once.

They are a group of beings inside me. This is not relationship. This is need fulfillment. The need so far inside me they pull it out like string.

We are the only ones here and still I left her. Still she left me.

I walk for days and hours and weeks. Alone. Alone again. Alone at the end. Nothing enough to keep us together and I miss her. Miss her in the way I used to miss her. Remembering when she asked me if I loved her or if I loved what loving her brought me, like how people saw it.

Walking amongst the rocks. Finding drawings. 1000 years, 2000 years. What we did to them. Where we find ourselves.

I thought loving her would protect me. I thought togetherness could exist. I guess it did. But what I wanted was belonging.

I hear a sound like water and follow it till a spot in the ravine shaded by rock. Drips of water collect. Little pools, filled with flies. I scoop water with my hands and pour it on my body.

I don't want to die alone.

Skin becoming thinner and softer, waves in my hands, wrinkles on my thighs, ripples where what was isn't anymore. Sun spots.

I don't miss her. I miss the way I was with her at the beginning. Feeling. All the feeling turned into dust.

Walking. Wandering. Open. Open to it.

Remembering her body. The way she sweats. The way she falls asleep with her mouth open. Her anger. Her bitterness. Hitting every note. Like the perfect meal

Scratching my scalp with twigs. Shaking out the dirt. Wishing for a blade or something to cut at the way it lengthens.

My first heartbreak, my mother. She tells me to leave the house, to never come back. I got used to leaving. People dying, people leaving, same thing repeated. Emptiness. No one to belong to in all the time spent afraid.

This heartbreak textured like all the rest but a real ending.

Endings like this don't usually exist. But here now there is no one else to love. No one else but me and dust and dirt.

I remove my clothes. Trusting the dirt. Trusting its mineral brown and orange. Rubbing my skin in it. Filling with it and squeezing it back out. A flexible entering, the way it opened me and smoothed. I pushed more and more in me till I expanded. It hurt to move. I waited. Rested. Feeling filled. Feeling air feeling sun on my skin. Warm and open. Temperature of the dirt inside me rising. The smell. The me that is earth, the me that is water.

I didn't recognize how much I hurt until I was really finally alone.

Holding myself till I feel warm. A hug. Wrapping my hands around me. I see a fox walk across the rocks.

Looking for something, not looking for me.

We drift. Alone.

Across.

What could be years.

Then the wind catches something of her, a hair in a coil, lands on my foot. She exists. She continues to exist.

I scream for her. I do not see her.

I scream. I scream. I sit in the dirt and I scream.

I fall asleep, sun on my face, burning.

I wake to a shadow.

Her face. Above my face.

You came back.

You came back.

I missed you. Every day.

I want to die with you.

I want us to do it together.

How to maintain love?

Make it like dust.

We are going to sleep and we choose to sleep next to each other.
I chose because I am in a remembering. So many died, so many
before us and around us and we are living and this is a burden.
Not quite regret but burden, yes.

She is holding me in her sleep pushing me further across the
endless rock. Her holding me, her smaller than me holding me.

Do you still love me?

Like are you in love with me?

Answer could be yes, answer could be I don't know.

What does it even mean anymore to be in love?

I'm startled by the need for you to love me.

Like the desire for there to be other people you could love
and you still choose me.

When she is sleeping holding me I feel myself get big and I
want to touch it afraid to touch it afraid she'll wake again and
I'll have to explain the desire the desire that is her the desire
that is fantasy of her the fantasy of holding her of leaving to go
somewhere else of missing you, of wanting to return to her the
fantasy of her never ends just changes like my body has changed

like the way the thighs grow out the way my pants stretch the way I needed the stress to avoid what was avoided I want so much from her she must feel it because she wakes a little moves her hand to my thigh she cannot see my face because she is holding me she grazes my thigh for minutes or seconds whispers in my ear

Are you awake?

I don't say anything at all I just take her hand and move it how I want it thinking about my vibrator before it died and the silicone squish of it how it looked like a peach swirl I move her hand slow then fast slow then fast trying to become vibrator pattern hand on the surface animate inanimate her hand her thigh her arm I pull in so she presses against me her hand hardening going inside me she feels my hips press into her move her further and further in asleep awake asleep awake I put a finger in her mouth she sucks it in showing me how it could feel if I opened enough her tentacle stroking inside.

If you put your finger up move it in the right direction you will hit a surface like a soft plate as you press into it it'll bounce back a little: there is where you push.

Her mouth her mouth a warm cavern her teeth melt away when she is on me.

We walk on roads till they lead to other roads wishing for a gas station with gas or anything inside any sort of memory but we find nothing just more and more roads then the road turns to sand and we stop following it.

Nothing looks new any more always the same alway the same not even music exists the sounds sometimes new but always in the same range staring at her reflection in water her seeing herself how many angles a face has.

Remembering mothers, sisters, friends. Friends died and we didn't know why, we didn't know how. Grief was a blanket. Grief threw us into the earth.

I wanted her to prove something to me so she took a lizard and made an incision down the belly flipped the lizard inside out scraped everything to the ground the skin a bowl for what I may find.

I wanted to prove something to myself so I slipped the knife
across my palm   blood bubbles.

I feel like I've been grieving you my whole life.

She's biting my finger trying to take it off reaches bone can't see the white because it's all red she wonders if my stomach would taste better cuts a piece off with a sharp rock lights a fire puts it on a stick the smell sweeter than we thought we take bites wondering what else, when desire ends it all ends.

Listening to the water knowing I need to become dirt.

We picked the spot on the hill. Hill looking over the brush, the crack in the dirt where water once ran through. We dug for weeks or months or years till we grayed.

Digging was hard when the tools we had were rocks, sticks.

Pushing the earth around, lining our grave with leaves.

Creating circles of grief. Circles like lines of topography.
Something beautiful, even here.

When the hole reached rock bottom we gathered grass. Arms
full. We filled our hole, making a cushion we did not make
ourselves in life. We tested it out, found comfort.

Stopped looking, started resting more. Stopped fucking, started holding.

Her body in mine, then my body in hers.

We wonder how long it'll take once we've stopped. We wait. A bird passes. Then a cloud. Then a star. We stare. We wait.

The way we wrinkled and drooped. Skin to skin. Body shutting down.

Like the way our mothers fell apart before us.

Days pass, my knees turn purple. It's cold here. Her breath rattles.

How much time since we stopped no way to know.

Death is arriving.

From our hole in the dirt I see spots like birds. Wind covered us with dust our circles becoming less distinct.

A fog, a dust, eyes leak, then dry.

Circles upon circles upon circles witnessing. All the times I felt disconnected. All of the times I felt completely alone. And here we are, together, connected, passing.

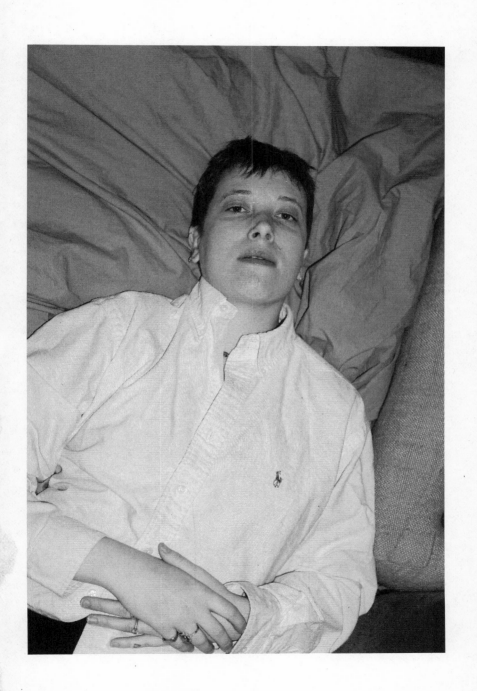

LA Warman is a poet, performer, and teacher currently based in New York City. Warman is the author of Whore Foods, an erotic novella which recieved a Lambda Literary Award in 2020. She is the founder of Warman School, a non-accredited and body based learning center. The Warman School has taught over 500 students online and in person. She teaches topics such as erotics, death, depression, and god. Pitchfork named her piece ADMSDP one of the top 100 songs of 2020. She has had performance and installation work in shows at MOCA Cleveland, ICA Philadelphia, Time-Based Art Festival, Poetry Project, and Open Engagement. Warman has presented performative poetics research at Brown University, Hamilton College, Reed College, Hampshire College, and others. She is a founding organizer of the Free Ashley Now survivor defense campaign.

Acknowledgements

I would like to thank all of my students at Warman School, for letting me learn from you. For everyone that has given me space & everyone who has held me. For Mitch my Forever Publisher for always giving me a chance. For Tamara Faith Berger for giving me the push I needed when I was stuck. Thank you to Sophie Mörner and Ainara Tiefenthäler for giving me places to stay and write. Thank you to Chelsea Hogue, Lillian Paige Walton, and Bridget Brewer for workshopping early versions of this book. For my cat Horse. For Cedar who showed me the desert. For my mentors and friends Arisa White, Lynn Xu, rev. angel Kyodo williams, S*an D Henry-Smith, Wilmer Wilson IV, Frankie Decaiza Hutchinson, Husna Kazmir, Natalia Panzer, Remy Maelen, K. Toyin Agbebiyi, Jamie Tyberg, Bhupali Kulkarni, Hoai An Pham, Callum Angus, Yolene Grant, Merray Gerges, and countless others. I am only what I witness. Thank you to everyone at the No Big Deal Sit for letting me witness you. Finding you all helped me find myself.